He   ts

Encoura   ew Moms

BY SANDRA BYRD

ILLUSTRATIONS BY SUSAN GROSS

WATERBROOK
PRESS

HEARTBEATS
PUBLISHED BY WATERBROOK PRESS
5446 North Academy Boulevard, Suite 200
Colorado Springs, Colorado 80918
A division of Random House, Inc.

ISBN 1-57856-326-7

Published in association with the literary agency of Janet Kobobel Grant, Books & Such,
3093 Maiden Lane, Altadena, CA 91001.

Library of Congress Cataloging-in-Publication Data
Byrd, Sandra.
    Heartbeats : encouraging words for new moms / by Sandra Byrd.—1st ed.
        p. cm.
    Includes bibliographical references.
    ISBN 1-57856-326-7
        1. Mothers—Religious life. 2. Postnatal care—Religious aspects—Christianity. I. Title.
BV4529.18.B97 2000
242'.6431—dc21

                                                                                00-022127

Printed in the United States of America
2000—First Edition

10 9 8 7 6 5 4 3 2 1

FOR MY CHILDREN,
SAM AND ELIZABETH

Once your hearts beat under mine.
Now we're side by side,
and my love for you is stronger than ever.

Contents

Adoration and Affection

I prayed for this child,
and the LORD has granted me what I asked of him.

1 SAMUEL 1:27

In the sheltered simplicity
of the first days after a baby is born,
one sees again the magical closed circle,
the miraculous sense of two people
existing only for each other.

—ANNE MORROW LINDBERGH

———

But Mary treasured up all these things
and pondered them in her heart.

—LUKE 2:19

Children and Other Dependents

Dawn slips above the shadowy horizon as we sit rocking, silence lightly peppered by the punctual tick of my watch. Elizabeth is almost finished nursing—her head relaxes and rolls back into the crook of my arm; her lips grow slack. Dependency came easily to her. From the very start she seemed to trust that things would work, latching on with the almost-painful pinch required to start the flow of the milk to her and the endorphins to me, never questioning that I would be there when she needed me.

Now she nods off for another dream while I struggle to stay awake without caffeine. A full day stretches ahead as I lay her down in the cradle that was once my sister's, caressing her angelic face. Quietly, I turn her on her side and pull the blanket up over her tiny shoulders, continuing the tradition of "tucking in" that my mother had started with me.

I scoot the chair next to the baby while I pump the other side for later, when I'm gone. Elizabeth is content, not thinking about the future or even the next hour. Like all babies, as soon as her immediate need is met, she finds everything right in her world. She breathes rhythmically in her gentle slumber. She doesn't need to worry or plan ahead. I'm doing that for her.

I fill one bottle, screw the lid on, and move to the next. The routine comforts me, pleases me, knowing I'm looking out for her while she sleeps. Even though she doesn't know it, I'm taking care of her needs way in advance.

Dawn gives way to morning; the light is whiter and stronger through the thin filter of drapes. Daytime is not as peaceful as dawn; my heart is unquiet. A week's worth of work threatens. How will I get everything done?

I pick up the Bible, hoping to catch a word of encouragement before I store the bottles and head to the shower. It falls open, but I can't focus. I close it again. I look down at the full bottles, the sleeping baby.

"God, please care for me, my day, my worries, just as I care for my child," I pray, feeling a little foolish even as I whisper. God loves me, adores me. He has prepared for my future way in advance, with more tenderness than I can imagine. A thought occurs: He wants me to be as dependent on him as Elizabeth is on me. Meal by meal, moment by moment. He wants me to be as filled with his peace as is a sleeping, trusting child whose needs are always met, who trusts that I will continue to meet her needs even when she can't see or feel me.

So often we get caught up thinking that we have to take care of everything, that without constant worry our fragile little lives will fall apart. They won't. Dependency means admitting that you are helpless in the face of a bustling world, but it also means living with the warm peace that comes from relying on God. In Isaiah 49:15 God proclaims, "Can a mother forget the baby at her breast and have no compassion on the child she has borne? Though she may forget, I will not forget you!"

Thank you, Father. You teach me more through my child than I could ever learn on my own. Help me to remember that you are ever mindful of me, that I never leave your thoughts, and that you are always looking out for my best interests. Help me to model that constant, attentive, and unconditional love to the little one who trusts me so completely. Amen.

Illumination

This is how you loved me, Lord.
You sent your sweet Son, your only Son,
Down here to get me.
He stretched out his arms for me, enfolded me,
Then took me back to you.
Watching over my vulnerable child I understand
Maybe for the first time
How much you love him, how much you love me.

—SANDRA BYRD

Father, so often I take you for granted, as if you exist to be at my beck and call. And I am angry when you don't. How embarrassing. But through this child you have given me, you remind me in a terrifyingly powerful way of the great sacrifice you made, asking your Son to set aside heaven and come down here as a baby to rescue me. You are holy. You are merciful. And your love is enough. Through his glory I pray. Amen.

Bathing Beauty...

What should I do next? I hear my mother in the other room, and I hope she stays there so I can figure this out without being self-conscious. I check the water temperature on the inside of my arm for the fourteenth time and twist the faucet away from the sink. The baby gazes up at me, his eyes as wide and wondering as my own. What if he slips? What if I drop him and he slides under the water? How can I wash his hair and still hold him with the other hand? I ease him in, gently settling his little bottom onto the foam pad. He draws in a breath and waves an adorable fist at me. He's smiling! I'm certain it's a smile! And I know I'm smiling.

1. Bathe baby (be sure to splash and have some fun!) and then wrap him in a soft towel.

2. Dry him off. Then lay him in the center of your bed, making sure he is comfortable, warm, and safe from rolling or squirming off.

3. Squirt a little warmed baby lotion into your palm.

4. Dip your third and fourth fingers (the weakest) into the lotion. Then lightly rub his shoulders and chest. Caress his skin with light circling motions; use no firm motion or pressure.

6. Massage slowly, working your way down his tummy and legs.

7. Roll him over—adding lotion as necessary—and massage his back and buttocks. You may also rub his hands and feet (they aren't ticklish yet!).

8. With a soft brush, gently brush baby's downy hair.

9. Softly massage baby's ears.

10. Dress him in something comfortable, and relax together. Savor the moment!

Baby Mine

In the coolness of the late night, old movies flicker blue and gray on the screen. I sit with the baby; he squirms in pre-sleep restlessness. It is true, after all. The TV is a new mother's faithful friend!

A symphony of snores from the next room tells me Michael is asleep. Devoted father, yes, but not at this hour. I glance at the shrink-wrapped video, *Dumbo,* perched on top of the television. What an odd baby shower gift—and from an experienced mother, too. It sits strangely among the diaper bags and onesies, the tiny cotton pullovers and velour animals. But nothing else is on at this hour, so watching *Dumbo* seems like a good option.

Sam stirs now, so I feed him with great hope that, as he becomes milk-drunk, he will nod off into a dreamless slumber. The movie begins, and the stork delivers bundles of bliss to many circus animals. Mrs. Jumbo waits expectantly. None arrives for her.

I know how that feels. The months of aching arms and an empty womb. Another Mother's Day in church, smiling outside, crying inside. Soon enough, though, just as Mrs. Jumbo has given up hope, the stork delivers. I smile. If only it were that easy! I stroke Sam's head. The red-blond fuzz, like the softest Chinese silk, greets my fingers.

The stork announces the arrival of a baby for Mrs. Jumbo. I smile with her, celebrate with her. I kiss Sam's cheek, chubby now, as a baby's should be. I adore him. I whisper grateful thanks to the One who sent him.

Snuggling and nodding off for a minute, I'm startled awake as Michael enters the room. "Are you coming to bed at all tonight?" he teases.

"Yes." I peel the burp rag from my shoulder. The scent of sour milk breezes by as I drop the cloth diaper onto the couch. "Do you know what?"

"No, what?" Michael asks, easing Sam from my arms. The baby's head droops, offering no help of its own; does he know his daddy will support him in all ways?

"I would know Sam's burp smell from any other baby's. It's uniquely his. And he's mine."

"You're hopeless," Michael says, kissing my cheek.

I stand in front of the television for another minute. The mother animals cuddle their babies to sleep—Mother Zebra and her striped little one, Mrs. Jumbo and Baby Dumbo. I click the TV off, smiling at the wisdom of this gift. Then I tiptoe in for one more nuzzle with my own Baby Mine.

Sometimes in our relationship with God, we have moments when we question. "Are you really there?" we ask. "Are you listening? Do you hear the cries of my heart?"

And then, in a beautiful way that only God can do, he answers.

I am here, he says. *I am listening. I hear the cries of your heart, and I care.*

Next time you wonder if your Savior is listening, lean over and brush your baby's cheek with a kiss. All things are made beautiful, in his time.

Dear, sweet Jesus, thank you for answering my prayers for this child. Like Hannah before me, I had been filled with both dread and hope, uncertain if I would ever hold my own child. Would everything turn out all right? And now, he's here, in all his soft glory. Remind me to treasure these late night moments and the quiet wisdom of the friends you scatter along my path. Amen.

Bonding

Your tiny fist clutches my finger
Squeezing, assuring you that I am here.

I am here.

I caress your hands, wondering what woman will take
      my place someday.
I kiss your fourth finger.
Surely she will too, as she slips her ring over it.

How few years I have with you.

What will your voice sound like?
What are you dreaming?
Your rosebud lips
Suck rhythmically, though nothing is there.

I lean to kiss you and wonder if it is worth the risk
Of waking you.
I kiss you, and together we sleep, for an hour
Or maybe two
'Til hunger rouses again.

—SANDRA BYRD

19

O Jesus, please help me to grab hold of these precious moments sifting through my fingers, to catch them and enjoy them before they disappear into the next minute and the next. Help me to slow down and savor this day that you have given to my child and me. Amen.

Guilt and Discouragement

My soul is downcast within me;
therefore I will remember you.

PSALM 42:6

Loose Threads

It is said that a day hemmed in by prayer seldom ravels
I'm praying, Lord, and I'm raveling
There is so much to do, and I don't know how to do it
What I do, I do wrong
I call out and I hear less than nothing, a vacuum
Are you there? Do you care?
Maybe this was a mistake; I can't be a good mother after all
Not a day goes by without a stumble, without a fall
Please take the loose threads of my life
Stitch them together
Hem me in behind and before
Knit together these raveling edges

—SANDRA BYRD

Neighborhood Secrets

I peeked at her every day, holding the slats on my miniblinds just right so the viewing space would be imperceptible. Certain as the morning paper, at ten o'clock she'd shepherd two nattily dressed preschoolers into a clean minivan.

I envied her gauzy dresses, loosely catching a whispered breeze. I wanted to feel pretty and feminine and put together again. I probably wouldn't wear wide-brimmed hats, woven of sun-bleached straw and cinched with a strawberry ribbon, but I might like to try. My car didn't need to be spotless, but the coffee cups rolling on the floor were talking of starting a union.

After a few minutes, I'd leave my post, go back to the television, back to the baby who was crying once more. I went into the kitchen to warm some tea, disgusted with the mess on the countertops…again.

Could every woman in the world except me juggle all these balls?

One day, more out of jealousy than curiosity, I pulled my hair into a ponytail and set the baby in her stroller. I made sure I was near my neighbor's step at ten o'clock. "Oh, hello!" I said, blushing slightly.

"How are you?" she responded, her lovely British lilt reflecting genuine pleasure.

"Fine, fine…" I said. "By the way, um, how do you three always get out so early looking great?" I had blurted it out. But she obviously knew what I meant.

"When Lizzie was born, I never got out the door until Reading Rainbow was over, and even then my house was a wreck," she chuckled. Hmm, I mused, that TV program ends at eleven o'clock. I wasn't usually ready until around noon, but at least I was within an hour of her schedule. Encouraged, I pressed on.

"And you always look so pretty." I gestured at her outfit.

"I started buying these dresses after I had the kids. Loose fit and all, you know," she pulled at the waistband and let it snap, showing me the stretch.

"What about your house?" I insisted, bugging her further, even though my brain was screaming, *Let it die!*

"Now that I have more energy it's not so hard to keep up." She saw my droopy eyes. "But the baby was at least six months old before I kept enough dishes clean to eat the next meal."

We chatted for a few more minutes, and she left to go wherever mothers of older children trundle off to on a peaceful summer morning. The baby and I strolled a bit and went home.

Later that evening Michael stayed with the baby while I went out to buy a crinkled, gauzy dress. When I returned, he'd made the kitchen sparkle. I think I can do this after all, I decided.

The seasons passed and another summer arrived. One day my nattily dressed child and I visited another neighbor, cooing at her new baby. We'd often chatted in the past, but I hadn't seen her since her baby had come. Her graying roots needed color; so did her complexion. She finally blurted out, "How come I'm the only woman who can't keep it together?"

"Let's sit down on the grass," I told her, "and I'll tell you a secret."

Thank you, Jesus, for reminding me that others have walked this path before me, and prevailed, and that I can too. Help me to keep open ears to listen to the chorus of encouragement you have placed around me but which so often, in my despair, I ignore. Remind me that all things happen within your good plan and that you will use my frustration as a soothing ointment for others if I will only allow you to do so. Amen.

---♡---

More than ever, now, I need to rely on the truth of the following verses to combat the many times I feel overcome with discouragement and lack of motivation to scrub one more crusty highchair tray, wash one more load of laundry (which is piled so high I think it's spontaneously regenerating) or stay in the house one more hour with a wailing baby.

What Is Postpartum Depression Like?

Approximately 80 percent of new mothers experience baby blues of some strength and duration, and 20 percent of all new mothers experience postpartum depression. If you are among that 20 percent, you are not alone. Neither are you weird, a bad mother, or faithless!

The onset of postpartum depression may occur during pregnancy, immediately after birth, or many months later. Moreover, the depression may occur with the birth of any child, not only the first, or after adoption.

Some of the common feelings and experiences are:

- I am so irritable
- I cry all the time or I feel like crying but I can't
- I can't get going/I can't slow down
- I feel so worried all the time
- I am scared—I am having panic attacks
- I can't feel anything
- I just can't cope
- I feel so alone
- I feel so guilty
- I feel so ashamed
- I don't know who I am anymore
- I can't sleep/I want to sleep all the time
- I feel so ugly
- I can't stop eating/I don't want to eat
- I don't want sex anymore
- I am having very scary thoughts

What Helps?

- Nurturing yourself
- Getting a break
- Finding childcare
- Developing a support system
- Getting sleep
- Accepting the painful feelings
- Coping with anxiety attacks
- Counseling

- Paying attention to good feelings
- Dealing with fantasies
- Finding coping strategies to deal with suicidal thoughts or feelings
- Taking one step at a time
- Doing something physical
- Keeping realistic expectations

—FROM *POSTPARTUM DEPRESSION AND ANXIETY: A SELF-HELP GUIDE FOR MOTHERS*,
PACIFIC POST PARTUM SUPPORT SOCIETY

When I first got postpartum depression, for months I didn't even know what it was. I'd never been depressed a day in my life—in fact, I wrote off those who were as wimps. Once I figured out what I was dealing with, I humbled myself and got help. There is no shame in being vulnerable, emotional, and interdependent. "Where there is no guidance the people fall, but in abundance of counselors there is victory" (Proverbs 11:14, NASB).

Yet this I call to mind
and therefore I have hope:
Because of the LORD's great love we are not consumed,
for his compassions never fail.
They are new every morning;
great is your faithfulness.
I say to myself, "The LORD is my portion;
therefore I will wait for him."
The LORD is good to those whose hope is in him,
to the one who seeks him.

—LAMENTATIONS 3:21-25

"For I know the plans I have for you," says the LORD.
"They are plans for good and not for disaster, to give you a future and a
hope. In those days when you pray, I will listen."

—JEREMIAH 29:11-12 (NLT)

30

Sack of Potatoes

*n*early a year into parenthood, I finally "got it." I began to understand the source of this heavy burden I nearly always carried around. You see, when I became a mother I apparently accepted an invisible—but readily accessible—backpack. And—with or without an invitation—lots of people felt free to contribute something…

"You're not feeding that baby whenever he wants, are you? He'll get spoiled."

"Are you letting him cry himself to sleep? His trust mechanism will be damaged."

"You're not holding him until he falls asleep! In a couple of months you'll be sorry you set up that pattern."

One pound of guilt.
It felt really heavy, though, because it was the first item to fall into the knapsack.

"Don't listen to the 'experts.' Listen to other mothers who have been there."

"Don't listen to other mothers. They're only going to tell you their own point of view. Read up on the latest research instead."

What about listening to myself?

Pounds two and three into the backpack. It was pulling on my shoulders a little now.

"Of course you're nursing. Why wouldn't you be?"

"You're not quitting nursing already, are you? Don't you know how good it is for the baby?"

"Are you still nursing? Isn't she a little old?"

Four pounds.

Was I doing something—everything—wrong? I'd check the books. I'd ask the doctor next time.

"Have you signed up for baby exercise classes? It's important for their muscle development."

"You're not putting out good money for those silly baby classes are you?

We never did those, and my kids are fine. You need to be more careful with your money now that you're a parent."

Pounds five and six.
The backpack straps were starting to pinch. All advice was well inten-tioned, I know. But trying to shift this pack around made me tired, and I was finding it harder and harder to know who was right.

"Going back to work? I thought you'd quit now that you have a family to take care of. Nobody can take care of a baby as well as its mother, you know."

"Shouldn't you be back at work? A growing family has lots of expenses, and you don't want to run yourselves into debt. Are you going to waste that education? And what about all the pressure on your husband to bring in all the money? It's a tight job market you know. Besides, what is there to do all day with a sleeping baby?"

Heavy guilt. We're up to ten pounds now.
A ten-pound sack of misshapen, potato-size balls of guilt that is never fully resolved.

"Are you opening that box of crackers in the store before you pay for it?"

"Does he still need a binky to fall asleep?"

"Do you know what disposable diapers do to the environment?"

Help, God! This is too much. I don't know what to do. I don't know whether what I am doing is right or wrong, and I don't know what you want me to do.

I sat, twisting my hands in my lap for an oddly quiet minute, and a passage of Scripture came flooding back. "Then Jesus said, 'Come to me, all you who are weary and carry heavy burdens, and I will give you rest. Take my yoke upon you. Let me teach you, because I am humble and gentle, and you will find rest for your souls. For my yoke fits perfectly, and the burden I give you is light'" (Matthew 11:28-30, NLT).

Ah, yes. I eased the backpack off and started pulling out the potatoes. I'd been too willing to accept everything that came my way, wanting to do the best for the baby and not knowing exactly how. But now I saw that if Jesus wants me to do something, he'll tell me. In fact, he had already told me, if I'd trusted myself to listen. I still consider wise and loving counsel from a few near to me. But I threw the backpack away. I wanted my shoulders to be free to carry his yoke.

Lord, help me to rely on you to tell me what is right, what is good. Help me look neither to the left nor to the right, comparing myself with other mothers to determine whether or not I am okay. Please prompt me to look straight up for inspiration and direction. Help me to hear the still, small voice of the Holy Spirit. Remind me to read the Bible, knowing that my firm foundation is laid in your excellent Word. Amen.

Understanding Guilt

Guilt is a common cause of depression. It is a form of pent-up anger, usually anger directed toward oneself.

There are two kinds of guilt. One is helpful; the other is harmful. True guilt—helpful guilt—attacks the specific, established wrong action. True guilt is the feeling of sadness and remorse over breaking a specific law—God's law, a moral law, or a civil law.

False guilt, however, attacks you, as a person, and makes harsh judgments about you as a human being.

Ask yourself: Have I broken a specific, definable law—biblical, moral, or civil?

If the answer is yes, ask for forgiveness from God and anyone else your actions affected, make restitution, and then forgive yourself. Don't expect yourself to be perfect. God doesn't. Modeling self-forgiveness is an invaluable lesson for your child.

False guilt is the feeling of dread that comes with committing a perceived wrong action. These perceptions often come in the form of "should" statements: "I should be more patient" or "I shouldn't have said that."

Such perceived wrongs stem from either our own inaccurate self-expectations or others' expectations of us. New mothers often think they "should be more...," "should do more...," or "should know how do to...," etc. The real danger with such false guilt is that it often leads to a generalized conclusion about oneself: "I am wrong"; "I am a bad person"; "I am a bad mother"; "I am not good enough."

Ask yourself:

1. Am I worried about what kind of mother others think I am? Do I constantly compare myself with other mothers?

2. Am I worried that my husband, mother, mother-in-law, or even I myself think that I am not a good enough mother?

3. Am I worried that others won't love and respect me for the choices I make?

If the answers are yes, perhaps you are inflicting unnecessary guilt on yourself due to unrealistic standards. Let them go. It's the first step toward enjoying peace and contentment.

—DRAWN FROM MATERIALS BY TIM SANFORD,
LICENSED PROFESSIONAL COUNSELOR AND AUTHOR

Joy and Contentment

You thrill me, LORD, with all you have done for me!
I sing for joy because of what you have done.

PSALM 92:4 (NLT)

Kitchen Dancing

The time? Midnight.

My gown? A fuzzy robe.

The music? A quiet radio.

The lighting? Dim glow of the digital clock.

My partner? A little bald man (only three months old).

We swing and sway in each other's arms as the night ticks by, oblivious to the rest of the world. My restless partner melts into my chest and we become one…again. Tonight I dream of a night on the town. Someday, my dreams will be of kitchen dancing.

—SUSAN ROCKWELL

My nighttime entertainment has changed considerably, along with the rest of my life. My days of late-night parties, midnight movies, and Denny's afterward are over for now, but I have replaced them with something more fulfilling than anything I'd known before. We sit together, our chair rocking on the worn linoleum, and I wonder, awestruck, at the gracious gift of this child.

Dear Lord, thank you for this baby, for changing the season of my life from one loveliness to the next. Please help me to remember that each day has its own charm, that each minute in time is something that will never be repeated. Help me not to wish away babyhood with its many trials and sleepless nights. Someday I'll wish them back. Amen.

Peekaboo

We sat on the floor, the two of us, me on one side of the newspaper and she on the other. Well, I sat and she wobbled, a pillow bunched up behind her back and two couch cushions keeping her upright.

I dropped the paper. "Peekaboo!" I said. She stared at me, wary. I pulled the paper up between us again.

"Peekaboo!" I called again, this time peeping around the corner of the paper.

At that moment I heard something; I remember it well. A hiccup? I looked closer and saw the big wide gums, and I knew what it was. A giggle. A real one!

I was hooked. From that minute on I knew no joy comparable to that of hearing my daughter laugh. I was on a mission, and I had the proper tools. I entertained her with squeaky ducks, key rings, crinkled tissue paper, or even my two hands, flat out in front of my face for peekaboo. No place or time was too embarrassing; no number of chuckles was enough to slake my thirst for the sound of it. And as her laughs grew longer and stronger, the motivation only grew more intense. We connected, she and I, in a new and exciting way, joy-bonding.

Late one night I lay in bed, dreamy, wondering what it was about her smile, her giggle, that fills me with sunshine. I think it is the fact that she is always happy to see me. I see it in her unabashed pleasure when I enter the room, her quick grin when I smile at her. And she's taught me an important lesson—perhaps the first of many she will teach me. Take pleasure in the small things, Mommy. Sharing a smile over a quick game of peekaboo is a gift—a single minute of delight. I recalled a quote by Thoreau, "As you spend your days, so you spend your life." My baby daughter reminded me that a joy-filled life is one that captures the small pleasures available to me each day.

Six Weeks Old

He is so small he does not know
The summer sun, the winter snow;
The spring that ebbs and comes again,
All this is far beyond his ken.

A little world he feels and sees:
His mother's arms, his mother's knees;
He hides his face against her breast,
And does not care to learn the rest.

—CHRISTOPHER MORLEY

Wonderfully Made

O LORD, you have searched me
     and you know me.
You know when I sit and when I rise;
     you perceive my thoughts from afar.
You discern my going out and my lying down;
     you are familiar with all my ways.
Before a word is on my tongue
     you know it completely, O LORD.

You hem me in—behind and before;
     you have laid your hand upon me.
Such knowledge is too wonderful for me,
     too lofty for me to attain.…

For you created my inmost being;
     you knit me together in my mother's womb.
I praise you because I am fearfully and
          wonderfully made;

your works are wonderful,
I know that full well.
My frame was not hidden from you
when I was made in the secret place.
When I was woven together in the depths of
the earth,
your eyes saw my unformed body.
All the days ordained for me
were written in your book
before one of them came to be.

—PSALM 139:1-6,13-16

Father God, I take such joy and pleasure in knowing that the very same hands that knit together my mother and my father, my husband and me, carefully crafted my child. Thank you for caring to make us, each one, wonderful in your sight, exactly as you want us to be. In Jesus' name. Amen.

My Mother

You painted no Madonnas
On chapel walls in Rome;
But with a touch diviner,
You lived one in your home.

You wrote no lofty poems
That critics counted art;
But with a nobler vision,
You lived them in your heart.

You carved no shapeless marble
To some high soul-design;
But with a finer sculpture,
You shaped this soul of mine.

You built no great cathedrals
That centuries applaud;
But with a grace exquisite,
Your life cathedraled God.

Had I the gift of Raphael
Or Michelangelo
Oh, what a rare Madonna
My mother's life would show!

—THOMAS FESSENDEN

Fingers and Toes

wo months pregnant; McDonald's for lunch…

"I forgot my vitamin today."

"Take it when you get home." Michael takes a bite of his Quarter Pounder with cheese. I drink my milk and eat a salad, gazing at his Coke.

"That might be too late. What if this is the exact date that spina bifida develops unless I take my folic acid?"

"Unlikely." He takes another bite.

"How do you know? You don't know, do you?" *Flash of brilliance.* "Aren't flour products fortified with vitamins and minerals?"

"Mmm-hmm." *Slurp.*

"I'm going to get a burger. I think the bun might help, at least until I get home to the vitamins."

Four months pregnant; driving home from the movies…

"I think I know what the problem is."

"What problem?"

I'm agitated now because he's clearly not concerned about this serious topic. Doesn't he care? "With the baby, of course!"

He looks over at me. "Did the AFP test show a problem?"

"No. But I still think there might be one." He's struggling to hide a smile. I sense rather than see it. I begin a slow burn toward anger.

"What kind of problem?"

"I think the baby could be a hermaphrodite."

"A WHAT?"

"Hermaphrodite. You know, not completely a boy or a girl. It's a problem in one in thirty thousand births. It could be us."

"Where did you read that? In your Pregnancy Paranoia book?"

I don't understand why he doesn't read the pregnancy books with me. "It's a good book!"

"All it does it get you worked up."

"Well, at least I'm aware of the problems."

"There are no problems."

I hope he's right.

Six months pregnant; after dinner at his parents' house…

"You know it will be your fault if the baby gets skin cancer."

"The baby's skin has never even seen sunlight. What are you talking about?"

"I don't mean now. I mean later. Look at all the redheads in your family. And the skin moles. Those are high-risk factors. We'll have to be awfully careful to keep sunscreen and a hat on all the time."

"I'll take total responsibility for my genetic deficiencies if the occasion arises."

He's hiding a smile again; I know it. Well, I'm not playing around. Skin cancer is the most common form of cancer in the country.

Eight months pregnant; in bed… He's been asleep for an hour, but not me. I wake him up.

"I need a banana."

He rolls over. "What?"

"I have leg cramps. I need a banana for the potassium."

He lumbers out of bed, gets the banana, and comes back.

I peel. "I went to the dentist today."

"Oh good. No cavities?" He mumbles. I give him a brownie point. He's not even complaining that I woke him up.

"Uh-uh. But another thought occurred to me."

"What?"

"You know the teeth on my dad's side of the family?"

"No, actually."

"Well, the front two teeth are really large. Not even braces can fix that. As far as I know, it's only the men who get them. But what if we have a girl and she gets them? She'll be subject to a lifetime of ridicule. They'll call her Beaver Girl."

"It will be okay."

I'm not convinced. He relieves me of the banana peel and we fall asleep.

Nine months pregnant; on the way to the hospital...

"The baby could have a serious birth defect."

"Yes, it could." He wasn't teasing this time.

"Then what?"

"Then we'll deal with it. It'll be okay. It's our baby, and we will care for and love it no matter what."

I don't answer, but I scoot a little closer to him on the truck bench. The pains are getting stronger and I don't have the energy to focus on my worries anymore.

Fifteen minutes old...

"He's beautiful!" Michael enthuses. He's just back from the baby's first bath, rushing to give me a report while I'm lying there, getting stitched up.

"Of course he is!" I smile, all pale-faced euphoria.

"I counted. They're all there," he reports.

"What are you talking about?"

"His fingers and toes. I counted, and they're all there. You've always been so worried about everything. I thought you'd want to know."

"Of course they're all there," I say, hiding a smile. *Silly dad.* Way down deep, I always knew the baby would be fine.

———

He will feed his flock like a shepherd.
He will carry the lambs in his arms, holding them close to his heart.
He will gently lead the mother sheep with their young.

—ISAIAH 40:11 (NLT)

I am the good shepherd.

—JOHN 10:11

It gives me such joy to think that, even now, when my primary responsibility is taking care of someone else (a relatively helpless someone else), Someone is tending to my needs with focused love and devotion. He's not only watching over my children, he's watching over and leading me!

The Lord's goodness surrounds us at every moment.
I walk through it almost with difficulty,
as through thick grass and flowers.

—R. W. BARBOUR

Fear and Insecurity

My mind reels; my heart races.
The sleep I once enjoyed at night is now a faint memory.
I lie awake, trembling.

ISAIAH 21:4 (NLT)

Chickpeas

Many days I feel fear washing over me, fear that I cannot protect my children from the multitude of dangers that await them in the world. Will some calamity overcome my children or me? Somebody could kidnap them; they could be in a car wreck (especially when I'm not with them...I don't know why, but that always seems scarier!); someone could hurt them when I'm not around. But just as I am protecting my child to the best of my abilities, my Father is protecting them and me, too. And his abilities are unlimited.

Focus

What a horrid, angry rash. Maybe I'm not changing her
        diapers soon enough.
        I'm responsible.
If she swallows something small, leans over the crib and falls,
        I'm responsible.
If she doesn't eat well enough, if her nails are clipped too close,
        I'm responsible.
I didn't read to her in utero, didn't buy Mozart for the Mind;
If she doesn't do well in school,
        I'm responsible.

"What are you focusing on?" said a friend who came alongside
        and put her arm around me.

"This baby giggles and coos, she smiles whenever she's smiled at.
        You're responsible.
"She has healthy, chubby thighs and pink-kissed cheeks.
        You're responsible.
"She cries because she misses you, stretches out her arms to you.
        You're responsible.

"She has a mat full of squeak toys, the biggest noise maker being her mom.
You're responsible.

"Let the other things go; you're a great mother."

Thanks, I needed that.

—SANDRA BYRD

Thank you, Lord, for my friends. Please help me learn to trust in your wisdom and theirs as I walk through this new garden of parenting, which has weeds as well as flowers. Help me to know which thoughts to pull out and let wither and which to shower with attention. Amen.

Two people can accomplish more than twice as much as one....
If one person falls, the other can reach out and help.

—ECCLESIASTES 4:9-10 (NLT)

A White Hen

A white hen sitting
    On white eggs three:
Next, three speckled chickens
    As plump as plump can be.

An owl, and a hawk,
    And a bat come to see:
But chicks beneath their mother's wing
    Squat safe as safe can be.

—CHRISTINA ROSSETTI

Jesus, I place my trust not in my ability to foresee and avoid all dangers, but in your all-seeing, all-powerful abilities, and your unfathomable capacity for love. Please help me to rest in the knowledge that everything is under your control. Thank you for caring not only for each little sparrow, but for my baby and me as well. Amen.

———

When you pass through the waters, I will be with you;
and when you pass through the rivers, they will not sweep over you.
When you walk through the fire, you will not be burned;
the flames will not set you ablaze.

—ISAIAH 43:2

A Tiny Tuxedo

Late on the fourth day, I willed myself to lay my baby down. I needed to leave the hospital for a few hours, or so they said. I picked up my purse, took out a brush, and looking in the mirror, pulled my dull hair into a ponytail. My eyes looked old.

Before leaving, I wandered back to the crib and touched the sterile steel rails jailing my son. No mobile playing a soothing lullaby. No bumper guards. No happy bunny wallpaper. Instead, cold fluorescent lights and antibacterial cleaners.

My husband, Michael, stood beside me, and fear, the ultimate stealth weapon, sneaked into the room unseen. I felt it wrap its evil arms around us both.

Something might happen while I am gone. I lifted Sam's tiny hand, his fingers limp and light in mine. He slept; blue veins crisscrossed eggshell eyelids. Thin IV tubes rushed medicine through the vein in his skull. I stared at it, remembering the afternoon the doctor slipped that needle in, and adrenaline chilled my blood.

"I'm sorry," he had said, agitated as well, "but the veins in his hands and feet are too small. They keep collapsing. We'll need to put the IV into his skull."

One member of the IV team stretched a large rubber band over his skull, and the veins throbbed angrily as the baby screamed in pain and confusion. Michael held Sam down; I couldn't. It was all unreal to me, and I stepped outside the room so I wouldn't pass out. I felt guilty about that. *I should have been there.*

"I guess I'll go now," I mumbled, returning to the present. I stretched my arms into my jacket sleeves.

"Where are you going?" Michael asked.

"I don't know. Not back to the house," I said. I didn't want to face the happy bunny wallpaper in silence. "Shopping, maybe."

The hallway echoed with the clomping of my boots as I walked toward the elevator. There were other sounds, too. The creak of wheeled cribs from treatment rooms to recovery rooms. The crunching of ice from a dispenser into the glass of a woman trying to keep her fluid levels up so she could nurse her daughter when they left the hospital. If they left.

Once I got into my car, it was a short drive to a little strip mall. Christmas lights twinkled in each window, pooling their reflections into the puddles on the ground like impressionist watercolors.

I drew a deep breath of the cool air and ordered a cinnamon coffee. Its strong scent roused me a bit. I wandered around in a few stores and bought a bear that flashed red lights and played Christmas carols when you squeezed its paws. *Sam will like that when he wakes up.*

Next door was a children's clothing store. I hadn't bought many clothes before his birth. People had said that the baby might be big, that I'd have too many clothes that wouldn't fit. They were right; Sam was big. It was a good thing, too. Big babies have a better chance of recovery. And he was only four weeks old.

As soon as I walked in, I saw it. A little velvet tuxedo—tiny, soft, and roomy. Festive. The salesclerk saw my longing. "Would you like this?" she asked. "It's the only six-month size left."

"I don't know," I said, backing out of the store.

I headed for a bench and sat down, its planks cool against my thighs. An outdoor sound system softly piped in Christmas carols, which surrounded me like a soothing cloak. What if I bought that tuxedo and Sam died? What if I had to take it home, unworn, and stare at it in the happy bunny room? *O Jesus, can I trust you with my son?*

The hopes and fears of all the years are met in thee tonight... As if on cue, perhaps God's cue, unseen carolers sang that familiar line through the sound system. Faith thawed my heart, flash-frozen by fear. I knew it was my answer.

Giving birth was the beginning of a joyous and precious and difficult and faith-requiring journey. As a mother, I saw that life offers both hope and fear. And both are met by the One whose birth into this world—as a fragile baby—would be celebrated soon.

My family would celebrate, I decided, with Sam in his new tuxedo. I crunched up the coffee cup, threw it away, and headed back to make my purchase.

Sam did recover from his blood poisoning, which had been the result of a tiny hole in his digestive system that hadn't closed all the way because he was delivered four weeks early (I was diabetic). And Sam wore his tuxedo for the holidays—and looked very smart in it, too!

Jesus, thank you that you promise to walk with me through the raging storms in my life, the fires that I am sure will consume me. But you hold them back. Please let me remember, next time there is a test, how gloriously you got me through the last one. Help me learn to be trusting and faithful. Amen.

Do not fear, for I am with you;
Do not anxiously look about you, for I am your God.
I will strengthen you, surely I will help you,
Surely I will uphold you with My righteous right hand.

—ISAIAH 41:10 (NASB)

Nerve Endings

I always thought that, if I tried hard enough, I could will away the physical symptoms that are the unwelcome gift of anxiety. I can't. But there are several helpful things you *can* do for body, mind, and soul that will diminish those aches and pains. Go ahead and try some of these suggestions. I promise they work.

BODY

Breathe deeply. Breathe in slowly, counting to ten as you do. Exhale slowly, again counting to ten. Repeat until you feel your natural breathing pattern slow down. This might take up to ten times.

Relax your muscles. While baby is sleeping or being watched by someone else for a few minutes, lie down in a quiet place. Close your eyes and, starting with your toes and moving up your calves, thighs, etc., tighten each group of muscles for five seconds. Then let them relax. Work your way up your entire body. Afterward, lie still for a few moments with your muscles as relaxed as possible.

Take a bath. Yes, with bath salts and candles. It really does work.

Exercise. Make some time for a brisk walk with the stroller or work out with an aerobics video while the baby sleeps. Exercise burns off adrenaline and leaves you feeling more peaceful for hours afterward.

MIND

Buy some comic strip books, like *Calvin and Hobbes.* They're short, they require little brainpower, and they get you laughing from the start.

Rent a great movie. Check out a chick flick or comedy and invite your best friend over to watch it with you. Laughing out loud and connecting with your friends stimulate endorphins.

SOUL

Meditate on Scripture. Once you've calmed the jitters, spend some time reading just one verse of the Bible. I usually choose the gospel of John, because I can read a single verse and think about it all day without having to tackle an in-depth word study.

Pray. Spend some time in conversation with God, even on the days you can't get a minute to yourself. He's near. He hears the whispered pleas.

Diamonds

I wanted a baby, dreamed of a baby.
Even when I was a small girl dressing Tiny Tina,
I knew I'd be a great mother, better than my friend
      Kristen, for sure.
Her doll always looked raggedy.

But now I'm not so sure I know what to do with this baby,
      a real baby.
I'm afraid I'm not a good mother, not good enough, anyway.
And I'm still looking at the Kristens around me.
How do their kids look? (Cleaner, of course.)
What do they do all day? (Stroll in the sunshine.)

I am afraid…
Of making a mistake that will harm her forever.
Of taking her out among too many people, and she'll
      get sick—
Or not taking her out at all, which will stunt her
      growth and her immune system.
Of dropping her when I bend over to pick something
      up (this happened last week).
That my tenderly nurtured dream was an illusion.

That everything I thought motherhood would bring,
      it won't.
I don't want to be afraid anymore.
I look down at her, beautiful, better than any cherished
      dream.
Motherhood is not cotton candy,
All sweetness that disappears with the slightest rain.
It is a diamond,
Made more beautiful by pressure
And presented with a flourish by Someone who loves me.
I prefer diamonds.

—SANDRA BYRD

Lord, thank you that the reality of motherhood that you created is better than any dreams I might nurture. Help me to be honest with myself, with others, and with you. Help me to recognize that you chose me to be this child's mother and that you will give me the ability to provide everything necessary for her well-being. Amen.

Like a crocus
       in the snow,
…I stand
       knee-deep in Winter,
holding
       Springtime
           in my heart!

—JOAN WALSH ANGLUND

I remember seeing the first crocus of spring, poking its head through the muddy slush thrown by the street plow onto the virgin snow of our front yard. Its purple head struggled through, somehow unaffected by the crusted, dirty blanket surrounding it. I want my life to be like that, faith struggling through, refusing to be buried by the avalanche of fearful possibilities.

Loneliness and Fatigue

God sets the lonely in families.

PSALM 68:6

A Cure for Loneliness

A mother at home not only takes on the multiple responsibilities of a management job, she inherits the problems as well. And perhaps the first well-worn business phrase she identifies with is, "It's lonely at the top." Much of what we do at home we must do "solo."…

Writing from Albany, Oregon, Penny Snyder makes these observations…

"When my daughter was born seven years ago, I marveled at all the aids available to mothers. I was surrounded by baby wipes, diaper services, tippee cups, and medicine for teething pain. There were strollers with attachments for diaper bags and diaper bags with attachments for everything else. I found child care books for every stage of development and toys of every size and shape.

"After two children and many baby wipes, I now know the most important aid for mothers.… The key to a successful and happy career as a full-time mother is not a device or a book, but a good friend.… Her understanding and support will get me through anything with a smile."

—JANET DITTMER IN
WHAT'S A SMART WOMAN LIKE YOU DOING AT HOME?

Dear Lord, please bring me some friends to share my joy and my pain. Let them be honest friends, friends I can share with truthfully, not having to pretend everything is perfect, friends who won't be scared away by honesty or make me feel foolish for talking. And help me be a good friend too. Amen.

God Will Take Care of You

Be not dismayed whate'er betide,
God will take care of you;
Beneath His wings of love abide,
God will take care of you.

Through days of toil when heart doth fail,
God will take care of you;
When dangers fierce your path assail,
God will take care of you.

All you may need He will provide,
God will take care of you;
Nothing you ask will be denied,
God will take care of you.

No matter what may be the test,
God will take care of you;
Lean, weary one, upon His breast,
God will take care of you.

—CIVILLA D. MARTIN AND W. STILLMAN MARTIN

Dry and Weary

O God, you are my God,
      earnestly I seek you;
my soul thirsts for you,
      my body longs for you,
in a dry and weary land
      where there is no water.

—PSALM 63:1

This is what the LORD Almighty, the God of Israel, says:
"I will refresh the weary and satisfy the faint."

—JEREMIAH 31:23,25

Lord, thank you for reminding me that in times of weariness and days of dryness you promise to refresh and satisfy me—if only I will seek that refreshment in you. Amen.

My Mommy Marathon
(or Why I'm Always Bone Tired)

Bed making, kitchen mopping
Try to squeeze in grocery shopping
Vacuum carpets on the hour
Pray for time to take a shower
Wash the dog—she's full of burrs
Who spilled syrup on her fur?
Open mail—oops, past due
Change another stinkeroo
Another snack? So glad for cheese
Even babies must learn, "please"
Kiss your sister, share your toys
Lipstick isn't for young boys
Swing the car's revolving door
Twenty errands, maybe more
Hurry, hurry, late for work
A paycheck's an important perk
Bread of idleness?
How could I munch?
I never get a chance for lunch!

—SANDRA BYRD

79

More Laundry

There was a time, not too long ago, when watching my husband undress at the end of the day sent a jolt of electricity through me. Tonight, as I watch him peel back the layers of business clothes, all I can think of is, *More laundry.*

I am so tired. Each and every thing lining up for attention in my day seems like just another item to conquer and cross off a never-ending to-do list. Some items, to be sure, will always remain chores: cleaning the bathroom, paying the bills, grocery shopping, going to the post office. But lately even once-pleasurable activities seem like chores too. Each task demands evaluation in the most calculating, least spontaneous way—even something that should be fun like playing with the baby. *Am I doing it enough? Have I spent enough time interacting with her today? And how far behind am I in my other tasks because of the time I* have *spent with her?*

I need to spend more time with my husband. Be sure to be his companion, the manuals tell me. That's a husband's greatest need and marriage insurance to boot. But I don't have the energy right now for a hand of cards, much less a round of golf. And the more I look at what I have to do, the deeper I feel myself sinking into a pit of the undone.

Help me, God.

The next morning, I pick up his clothes, still scattered on the bedroom floor. I stuff them into the hamper before starting on the day's chores. My eyes can barely focus from fatigue, and I am already daydreaming about catching a few winks.

I pick up the baby and put her in the swing while I clear the kitchen counter. I glance up above the sink at the picture hanging on the wall. Thunderclouds hover over a rolling prairie, and the stalks of wheat are bending to the storm's powerful wind. But in the background, a sun-speckled patch of wheat is lit by a rainbow cutting through the lightening sky. The caption says, "This too will pass."

I smile in spite of my aching bones, which feel sponge-like and weak from lack of sleep. Elizabeth giggles in the swing, sucking on a chubby fist and babbling at me as I talk with her. I glance at the stack of movies Michael has rented for tonight—including an Emily Brontë–inspired flick. For me.

At times the cost of building a family is exacted in weariness and more laundry, for now. *Count the cost,* I remember. And then—*this too shall pass.* I can pay attention to a baby in a swing while I load the dishwasher, and I can be a companion to my husband while watching a movie, for now. Number one on today's to-do list: Take a nap.

Dear Lord, I am weak. I am weary, exhausted. I can barely keep my eyes focused, and I am afraid that I will fall asleep while I am driving or when I am supposed to be watching the baby. Please see my troubles. You say that you do. Thank you for hearing my case. Give me new strength to make it through this day. Please help the baby to nap well this day so that I can too. Help me to have the courage to say no to anything other than rest. And please help the baby sleep just an hour or two longer tonight. Thank you for always caring and for miraculously providing for me in big and small ways. In Christ's name I pray. Amen.

"I saw a sign: 'Rest Area 25 Miles.'
That's pretty big. Some people must be really tired."

—STEVEN WRIGHT, COMEDIAN

*If we visited that rest area,
I'll bet we'd find lots of new mommies.*

Wisdom and Understanding

*Happy is the person who finds
wisdom and gains understanding.*

PROVERBS 3:13 (NLT)

Wisdom

Dear brothers and sisters, whenever trouble comes your way, let it be an opportunity for joy. For when your faith is tested, your endurance has a chance to grow. So let it grow, for when your endurance is fully developed, you will be strong in character and ready for anything.

If you need wisdom—if you want to know what God wants you to do—ask him, and he will gladly tell you. He will not resent your asking.

—JAMES 1:2-5 (NLT)

Jesus, sometimes I wonder if I am up to the task of mothering. Thank you that I can come to you with all my questions (Should I use cloth diapers? Is it time for solid foods? Will this person watch my child well?) and know that you do not resent my asking. Instead you want to share your wisdom and love and strength. Lord, give me wisdom every day, as I seek to guard this little one's health and happiness and to raise him to love and serve you. In Christ's name. Amen.

Three Little Words

One day when my baby was a few months old, I went shopping. Not alone, mind you, but at least I was out of the house.

Amidst the clutter and knick-knacks at my local gift shop, I spied the cutest plaque. It said, "Say the three little words I long to hear—'Let's eat out!'"

Later, when talking with my girlfriends, we agreed that although "I love you" was still the most important three-word phrase, adding children to our lives made some other three-word combos nearly as appealing.

I decided to see what we could come up with that meant just as much as—well, almost as much.

SHERRI'S LIST

- I'll change him.
- I'm coming home!

JANE'S LIST

- Sleep in, honey.
- Take it easy!
- Kick back, relax.
- How are YOU? (not, "How is the baby?")

SANDY'S LIST	MY LIST
• The sitter's here!	• Take a nap.
• You look nice!	• Today is payday.
• Can I help?	• Your mom's coming.
• They're both asleep. (Sandy has twins.)	• You're doing great!
• The coffee's ready.	• You've lost weight.
• I'll cook tonight.	
• I'll do dishes.	

And everybody's favorite…I'LL GET UP!

Wisdom is as the morning light
…a gradual illumination.

—JOAN WALSH ANGLUND

———

A good mother is like a good quilt:
She warms her children, but doesn't smother them.

—UNKNOWN

Left Behind

Some people see conspiracies behind every door. Not me. I'm usually a hard-nosed reality buff. But this time I knew something was up.

"Here's a gift certificate." My mother handed me an envelope emblazoned with gold loops and swirls. "I've made reservations for you two for Saturday night."

"Hmm." I shifted the baby into one arm and pulled out the card. Fancy restaurant downtown. "I don't think they allow kids. Not babies, anyway."

"Right," she said, catching the baby's fist with her finger, to his delight. "He can stay with Dad and me."

Poor kid. He was gurgling in bliss, not knowing that plans were being made and he'd be Left Behind.

I looked up at her and rolled my eyes, but before I could say anything else my husband leapt in with, "Thank you. We'll look forward to it." He didn't look at all surprised, and my intuitive nature sensed he knew this was coming. I stared, trying to catch a wink between them, but I didn't see any giveaway clues.

I hadn't yet left the baby with anyone. I mean, why should I? He'd have the rest of his life to be away from me. No one could care for him like I could. They wouldn't know which burp meant "More please" and which meant "I'm full." I hadn't even left him at the nursery at church; instead, I took him with me into the sanctuary. We sat in the back, although lately he'd been raising a fist and shouting out his version of "Amen!" a bit too loudly, which was turning into a problem.

But I wasn't sure that those women in the nursery could handle all the babies. Besides, did they really disinfect those changing tables? They say they did…

So, I got my hair cut, found a dress that would zip up the back if I held my breath, and put on the first pair of semi-high heels I'd worn since my last job interview.

I was ready to go out on the town.

When we left him, the baby was fast asleep in the center of my parents' huge bed. My mom promised to sit right next to him. So we left, and he was Left Behind.

I don't remember what I ate. I remember what I talked about, though.

"What if my dad wants ice cream?" I asked as Michael dug into his dinner with enthusiasm.

"What if?" he said.

"Well, they might not have any, and then they might think it would be

90

nice to take the baby for a ride. And then they could get into a car crash, and the hospital wouldn't know where to find us."

"I have a pager," he reminded me.

"What if they're unconscious?" I pressed on.

"It'll be okay," he said. But I noticed he ate with less gusto.

I picked at my food. "What if my mom has to answer the phone and leaves the baby alone on the bed and he rolls off?"

"She won't leave him, will she?" he asked.

"I don't think so, but I don't know. She seems so relaxed about this whole thing. Too relaxed, really."

The waiter came, concerned that I didn't like my food. I ordered dessert just to please him. "What if the baby wakes up and thinks I've abandoned him?" I asked. "And you aren't there either!"

"I don't know." Michael gulped his coffee. We finished up and got into the car.

"It feels strange not to have the baby in his seat," he said. "Like we've left him somewhere."

"We have," I answered. But now that we were on the way home, I felt better. I allowed my hand to steal across the seat and took Michael's hand in mine. We felt like a couple again, if only for a few minutes.

"Maybe we should put him in the nursery tomorrow," he suggested. "You could leave them specific instructions to get us if he cries."

"Okay. We can try it anyway," I agreed.

We pulled up in front of my parents' house, and I jumped out almost before the engine was shut off. I ran up the steps and cautiously opened the door. All was quiet.

My dad sat on the couch, eating ice cream. My mom was in her bedroom, still sitting in the same chair as when I'd left. And Sam was on the bed, sleeping.

"Did he wake up?" I asked.

"Once. I fed him and changed him and he went right back to sleep. I don't think he knew you were gone."

"Oh." I said, relieved and slightly disappointed at the same time. "Well, we'd better get going." I gathered the diaper bag and wrapped Sam in his Snugli. *I might as well ask.* "Were there any problems?"

"Well, one," she admitted. *I knew it. I knew it!*

"Could you drop this into the garbage on your way out?" Mom smiled and handed Michael a dirty diaper, double wrapped in a plastic bag. "I forgot how badly they stink. I wouldn't want it Left Behind."

When we first become mothers, we think we can't do anything right. I remember being so humiliated when I couldn't stop my baby's crying, but the maternity nurse knew just how to pat him to relieve his gassy tummy. Feelings of embarrassment and incompetence flooded over me. My fear of being inadequate soon turned, however, into the unshakable belief that only I could care for my child. No one else would do. As I have grown and trusted and sought capable hands to help me, I've learned that God has placed willing and loving hearts all around my children and me. With wise discernment, I can find others to help me care for my gems.

Father, thank you for giving me other people who love my child, who welcome the privilege of helping me care for him. Help me to trust in their goodness and to know deep in my heart that you are guiding me as I seek whom to leave my child with when I must be away. I am glad I am growing as a person and as a mother, as I learn to trust my child to your protective hands. Amen.

A Cradle Song

I kiss you and kiss you,
My pigeon, my own;
Ah, how I shall miss you
When you have grown.

—W. B. YEATS

Acknowledgments and Permissions

All materials not cited here are the original work of the author.

ADORATION AND AFFECTION

Quote by Anne Morrow Lindbergh. Reprinted from *Gift from the Sea,* copyright 1955, 1975. Used by permission of Pantheon Books, a division of Random House, Inc.

GUILT AND DISCOURAGEMENT

"What Is Postpartum Depression Like?" Adapted from *Postpartum Depression and Anxiety: A self-help guide for mothers,* copyright 1987, 1997. Used by permission of the Pacific Post Partum Support Society (www.postpartum.org).

"Understanding Guilt," materials used by permission of Tim Sanford, licensed professional counselor and author.

JOY AND CONTENTMENT

"Kitchen Dancing" by Susan Rockwell, copyright 1991. This poem is reprinted from *Discovering Motherhood,* published by Mothers at Home, with the permission of the author and Mothers at Home, Inc. For a free information package about Mothers at Home and its publications, please call toll-free 1-800-783-4666. You may also write to MAH, 8310A Old Courthouse Road, Vienna, VA 22182, or visit their Web site at www.mah.org.